THINK ON THESE THINGS

THINK ON THESE THINGS

A Study of Philippians 4:8

GWENDOLYN HARMON

Learning Ladyhood Press

For Lorry and Ruth

Contents

Introduction: Gaining Control of our Thoughts

The Bible has much to say about the importance of our thinking. Perhaps the most fundamental truth concerning our thinking is found in Proverbs 23:7, which says,

"For as he thinketh in his heart, so is he. Eat and drink, saith he to thee; but his heart is not with thee."

This verse is found in the midst of an illustration about a rich man's grudging hospitality, but it is a good summary of the importance of our thoughts. As we think, so we are.

Our thoughts define not only what we do and how we feel, but even who we are, or at least, who we think we are. Our very concept of self-identity can be changed just by changing how we think about ourselves and the world.

But as we will see, this is why it is so important that our minds be taught to dwell on God's way of thinking, not our own. The God who made us, who designed every aspect of our being, is the God who has already and irreversibly defined our true identity.

By learning to think upon that which is true, honest, just, pure, lovely, of good report, virtuous, and praiseworthy, we free our minds and hearts from that which seeks to obscure, confuse, or obliterate our true identity in Christ.

This idea of submitting our thinking to God, of yielding our hearts and minds to the truth of who we are in Him, will likely trigger an instinctive reaction from our flesh. You may even want to throw this book across the room after reading that last paragraph, or perhaps you just have your head cocked, your eyes narrowed in suspicion of this idea of changing your thinking and identity.

But however the world, the flesh, and the devil may fight the truths in this book, my prayer for you is that you will choose to embrace truth, to lean upon God's Word instead of your own understanding *(Proverbs 3:5)*, that you may experience the blessedness of rooting your thoughts, emotions, actions, and identity in God.

"Finally, brethren, whatsoever things are true, whatsoever things are honest, whatsoever things are just, whatsoever things are pure, whatsoever things are lovely, whatsoever things are of good report; if there be any virtue, and if there be any praise, think on these things."
Philippians 4:8

I

True

"Finally, brethren, whatsoever things are true, whatsoever things are honest, whatsoever things are just, whatsoever things are pure, whatsoever things are lovely, whatsoever things are of good report; if there be any virtue, and if there be any praise, think on these things."

Jesus said, *"I am the way, the truth, and the life: no man cometh unto the Father, but by Me." (John 14:6)* A study of any aspect of the Christian life must begin here: with salvation. The truth of salvation is the most fundamental truth, succinctly stated in 1 Timothy 1:15, where Paul (inspired by the Holy Spirit) declares,

"This is a faithful saying, and worthy of all acceptation, that Christ Jesus came into the world to save sinners; of whom I am chief."

Paul knew perhaps more than anyone the power of God to save even the vilest sinner, for he himself had been instrumental in the persecution and murder of some of Christ's own followers—and still Christ forgave him fully and freely!

This forgiveness was not an exception, either. When the Pharisees reviled Jesus for eating with "sinners," He replied by saying,

> *"They that be whole need not a physician, but they that are sick. But go ye and learn what that meaneth, I will have mercy, and not sacrifice: for I am not come to call the righteous, but sinners to repentance." (Matthew 9:12-13)*

In the book of Romans, we are told many true things regarding salvation. The first is that none of us can be "good enough" for heaven, *"For all have sinned and come short of the glory of God." (3:23)* It only takes one sin to make you and me into sinners, separating us from God, who is perfectly holy and just. And yet, that is not the only truth about salvation.

We are all sinners in need of the Savior, but how wonderful to think upon the next truth, that God loves us, even in our sin! Romans 5:8 tells us,

> *"But God commendeth His love toward us, in that, while we were yet sinners, Christ died for us."*

While we were yet sinners, incapable in ourselves of bridging the gap between ourselves and God, Christ demonstrated His love by dying a painful and humiliating death in order to pay the penalty for that sin. He bridged the gap with His own suffering and death so that we could have the opportunity to accept His payment for sin and be brought into eternal fellowship with God. Jesus puts it this way in John 3:16,

> *"For God so loved the world, that He gave His only begotten Son, that whosoever believeth in Him should not perish, but have everlasting life."*

Salvation is freely offered out of God's heart of love for mankind. One of my favorite descriptions of how salvation works is found in 2 Corinthians 5:21.

"For He hath made Him to be sin for us, who knew no sin; that we might be made the righteousness of God in Him."

You see, it was the sinlessness of Christ that made it possible for Him to pay for our sin. He willingly bore the righteous wrath of God—wrath that *we* deserved for our sin—so that you and I could have our sins forgiven and be given the righteousness of Christ instead.

Truth's Definition

John 18 records that, as Jesus stood before Pilate prior to His crucifixion, Pilate had an exchange with Jesus from which he turned with a remarkable question:

"What is truth?" (v.38)

Sadly, Pilate left without waiting for the answer, and never accepted the fact that *the* Truth had been standing before him—though he freely admitted that he could find no fault in Jesus, and had been afraid when the Jews told him that Jesus had claimed to be the Son of God. (18:38, 19:8)

A study of all the true things in Scripture would be a work of massive scope, because the Bible *is* truth. A good application for us is the simple fact that God's instruction to think upon things that are true means first and foremost to think upon His Word.

But what about this word *true* in Philippians 4:8? Can its definition shed any light upon what exactly God wants us to fill our thinking with? This question always prompts me to pull out my *Strong's Concordance*, or my Bible app, which has Strong's and Thayers' definitions built in. The

Greek word used in this verse literally means "not hid." I can think of a couple of applications to this in reference to our thinking:

The Secret Things

This concept of things that are not hidden reminds me of Deuteronomy 29:29, which says,

"The secret things belong unto the Lord our God: but those things which are revealed belong to us and to our children for ever, that we may do all the words of this law."

The context of this verse is Moses' instructions to the nation of Israel as they prepared to go into the Promised Land. This verse comes in the middle of a passage dealing with the seriousness of the covenant they were entering into with God, and the fact that God would indeed bring judgment if they forsook the covenant. The "things revealed," therefore, are the truths of Scripture, the statutes, principles, and commands we are to follow.

I don't know about you, but I like to solve things, especially anything resembling a mystery. This can be a real danger to us as Christians. As the first part of this verse indicates, there are some things God has not chosen to reveal to us in Scripture. These "secret" things can become a real stumbling block to us if we allow our minds to get focused on them.

In 1 Timothy 6, Paul, through the Holy Spirit, ends a section of teaching by warning Timothy,

"If any man teach otherwise, and consent not to wholesome words, even the words of our Lord Jesus Christ, and to the doctrine which is according to godliness; He is proud, knowing nothing, but doting about questions and

strifes of words, whereof cometh envy, strife, railings, evil surmisings, Perverse disputings of men of corrupt minds, and destitute of the truth, supposing that gain is godliness: from such withdraw thyself." (vv.3-5)

When we choose to fix our minds upon *"questions and strifes of words"* instead of on the clear truths revealed in Scripture, we often get drawn into envy, strife, and even bitterness or hatred of those who have a differing opinion. As much as we need to understand, stand upon, and stand for the truths of Scripture, there are many "mysteries" over which we do not need to be drawn into debate, because no matter what opinion we choose to hold on the issue, God has not revealed enough to us to hold a definitive position based on Scripture.

I say all this because as we learn and grow in our understanding of the Bible, it is easy to get prideful and puffed up in our own opinions, or to fill our minds with one specific teacher's writings, and allow those things to fill our minds to the point of pushing the Word of God itself out of our minds completely. This is dangerous ground, because it leaves us vulnerable to false teaching and prevents our true spiritual growth: not just in knowledge, but in Christlike character as well.

While we are not responsible for the things God has chosen not to reveal, we *are* responsible for the things He has already made known. We are to think upon those things.

Thoughts Revealed

Another aspect of our thinking having to do with things that are "not hid" is perhaps a bit more of a stretch, but helpful, nevertheless. We are to think upon things that are not hidden, but as Christians, our thoughts should dwell on things that *need not* be hidden.

How embarrassed would you be if the people around you could hear what you were thinking? And yet, we so often forget that God Himself knows our every thought.

"He that planted the ear, shall He not hear? He that formed the eye, shall He not see? He that chastiseth the heathen, shall not He correct? He that teacheth man knowledge, shall not He know? The Lord knoweth the thoughts of man, that they are vanity." (Psalm 94:9-11)

As we strive to conform our thoughts to the pattern of truth provided throughout Scripture, we must do so remembering that God knows, sees, and hears, all.

* * * *

So how about you today? Are your thoughts focused on the revealed truth of Scripture? Or are they characterized by puffed-up opinions or thoughts you feel must be shamefully hidden away? Whatever the Holy Spirit is pointing to in your thinking today, yield to His conviction and guidance. Take your thoughts captive and choose only to think on whatsoever is *true*.

2

Honest

Finally, brethren, whatsoever things are true, whatsoever things are honest, whatsoever things are just, whatsoever things are pure, whatsoever things are lovely, whatsoever things are of good report; if there be any virtue, and if there be any praise, think on these things.
Philippians 4:8

At first glance, true and honest may appear to be basically the same thing. After all, when we talk about being honest, we're usually referring to telling the truth. But this is where I find it helpful to look at what the original Greek word means.

The word here for *honest* is translated appropriately, but in the older sense of the word, that of being worthy of honor. In fact, the Greek word for *honest* comes from another word meaning to revere or adore. God is telling us that we are to fill our minds with that which is worthy of honor or reverence.

This word appears three other times in Scripture, each of which has been translated as "grave."

"Likewise must the deacons be grave, not double-tongued, not given to much wine, not greedy of filthy lucre; Holding the mystery of the faith in a pure conscience." (1 Timothy 3:8-9)

"Even so must their wives be grave, not slanderers, sober, faithful in all things." (1 Timothy 3:11)

"But speak thou the things which become sound doctrine: That the aged men be sober, grave, temperate, sound in faith, in charity, in patience." (Titus 2:1-2)

Notice a common theme here? Those who are mature in the faith are to be grave, or honest in the sense of being worthy of honor, honorable. How we think determines what we do, so if we want to be Christians who are known to be honorable, we must think upon honorable things.

Of course, there is nothing more worthy of honor and reverence than God Himself! Psalm 66 gives just a glimpse of what a heart dwelling on the honor of the Lord will dwell on:

"Make a joyful noise unto God, all ye lands:
Sing forth the honour of His name: make His praise glorious.
Say unto God, How terrible art Thou in Thy works! Through the greatness of Thy power shall Thine enemies submit themselves unto Thee.
All the earth shall worship Thee, and shall sing unto Thee; they shall sing to Thy name. Selah.
Come and see the works of God: He is terrible in His doing toward the children of men.
He turned the sea into dry land: they went through the flood on foot: there did we rejoice in Him.
He ruleth by His power for ever; His eyes behold the nations: let not the rebellious exalt themselves. Selah.
O bless our God, ye people, and make the voice of His praise to be heard:
Which holdeth our soul in life, and suffereth not our feet to be moved.

For Thou, O God, hast proved us: Thou hast tried us, as silver is tried.
Thou broughtest us into the net; Thou laidst affliction upon our loins.
Thou hast caused men to ride over our heads; we went through fire and through water: but Thou broughtest us out into a wealthy place.
I will go into Thy house with burnt offerings: I will pay Thee my vows,
Which my lips have uttered, and my mouth hath spoken, when I was in trouble.
I will offer unto Thee burnt sacrifices of fatlings, with the incense of rams; I will offer bullocks with goats. Selah.
Come and hear, all ye that fear God, and I will declare what He hath done for my soul.
I cried unto Him with my mouth, and He was extolled with my tongue.
If I regard iniquity in my heart, the Lord will not hear me:
But verily God hath heard me; He hath attended to the voice of my prayer.
Blessed be God, which hath not turned away my prayer, nor His mercy from me."

It's a lengthy psalm, but notice the high regard the psalmist has for God. When we train our minds to dwell on who God is and what He has done, we will not be able to keep from singing and speaking His praises, both inwardly and before others.

Of course, the very best way to fill our minds with thoughts of God is to memorize and meditate on Scripture. Memorization is important because the repetition and time spent on the individual words and phrases cause us to pay more attention to what God is communicating through His Word.

Another practical way to fill our minds with thoughts of who God is and what He has done is to read about His working in the lives of other believers. As I write this, I have just finished reading a stack of biographies of missionaries and other Christians whom God has used to do amazing things for His sake.

I have found myself more than once in the last few weeks recounting to a fellow believer one of the ways in which God particularly worked on behalf of one of these faithful servants of God. When you fill your mind with the mighty works of God, you will naturally speak of those things to others, which ends up being an encouragement to you and to those around you!

It is so easy to focus on the negative things in life. But God makes it clear in Philippians 4:8 that we are to think upon those things that are honorable, worthy of honor. May we be the kind of Christians who live out the example of 1 Timothy 3 and Titus 2; Christians who are honorable because we have filled our minds with thoughts of God, delighting in who He is and what He has done.

3

Just

"Finally, brethren, whatsoever things are true, whatsoever things are honest, whatsoever things are just, whatsoever things are pure, whatsoever things are lovely, whatsoever things are of good report, if there be any virtue, and if there be any praise, think on these things."
Philippians 4:8

As I researched this concept of things that are "just," I noticed several individuals who are described in Scripture as being just. There is Joseph of Nazareth (Matthew 1:19), John the Baptist (Mark 6:20, Luke 1:17), Simeon (Luke 2:25), Joseph of Arimathea (Luke 23:50), and Cornelius (Acts 10:22). Each of these men is described as being *just*. But what exactly does that mean?

This word is tossed around much these days in the form "justice" or its opposite, "injustice." In the Greek, the word for "just" in Philippians 4:8 not only has this idea of judicial justice or equity, but also implies justness or righteousness before God. Look again at the list of men the Bible calls just. Each one has this same thing in common: each was primarily concerned with doing what was right.

Joseph wanted to do the right thing when he found out that his betrothed, Mary, was with child. Instead of exacting vengeance, he desired to show mercy.

John the Baptist was known for being bold with the truth, especially concerning sin and the need for repentance. He is known for pointing people to the Messiah and was eventually martyred for speaking out against the blatant sin of Herod. (Mark 6)

Simeon was a man close to God. He is described as devout, and waited expectantly for the fulfillment of God's promise that he would see the Messiah before he died. We know that he was led by the Holy Spirit to visit the temple the day he met Jesus there, and through the Holy Spirit he not only proclaimed that the baby in his arms was God's promised Savior, but also foretold His future rejection by many and the sorrow Mary would experience as she watched the crucifixion about 33 years later.

Joseph of Arimathea was a member of the Sanhedrin who had been a secret follower of Jesus. He is described as a good man, and it is also said of him that he waited for "the kingdom of God" ushered in by the Messiah. He is best known for appearing before Pilate to ask for the body of Jesus after the crucifixion.

This was a bold move for one who had thus far kept himself distanced from Jesus, at least in public. His own council had urged Pilate to crucify Jesus, and by asking for His body, Joseph risked the suspicion and possibly retribution of both the Roman authority and his own people. He put his reputation, his position on the Sanhedrin, and possibly his life on the line in order to do what was right.

Cornelius is an interesting case, because he is the only Gentile referred to as "just." He did not know Christ when this was said of him, but was doing all he could to seek after God, though he had not yet heard of the Savior. A Roman centurion, Cornelius is called a "devout" man, who prayed "always" and gave money to the poor. It was this man God chose to be the catalyst of the first proclamation of the Gospel specifically to the Gentiles.

To be a servant of the Jew's God as a Roman soldier must have been risky, particularly since the Romans were the ones who had executed Christ's death sentence, and, as a whole, were not known for being favorable to the Jews. Yet this man not only obeyed the instructions given him by the angel *(Acts 10:3-6)*, but also invited all his family and close friends to come and hear the gospel. *(v.24)* He was a man known for seeking God, a man bold to invite others to seek God with him.

Part of filling our minds with things that are just is noting the example of those around us who are steadfastly focused on doing right, whatever the cost. There is much we can learn from the Corneliuses and Josephs in Scripture as well as in our lives today.

God's Justice

Of course, we can also fill our minds with the truths of God's Word concerning the justice of God. This is one reason it is helpful to read the Bible cover-to-cover. It gives us an understanding of the overarching story of history from God's perspective, and also gives us insight into who God is, what He is like, and what is important to Him.

Growing up in a Christian home, I knew that Bible reading was important, but my own immaturity and lack of accountability made it difficult to stick with the various reading plans that came across my way. Graciously, God sent me to a new piano teacher when I was in my early teens. This teacher not only "assigned" her teenage students to read through the Bible, she gave us the accountability needed to help us succeed in it, as well as help with developing our study skills so that we understood more of what we read. I don't know what this did for the other students, but for me, it was just what I needed to get serious about daily Bible reading.

Don't get me wrong: I didn't suddenly become a flawless example of faithfulness in God's Word, but I did start to shake the sense of helplessness and discouragement that had made me want to stop trying. And the more I read, the more I understood; and the more I understood, the more I really began to get to know God. As I began to get to know God, I began to see my Bible reading, not just as a duty or an academic exercise, but as a precious time when God actually spoke to me through His Word.

It was in the midst of this process of growth (which, perhaps, never really ends) that I "discovered" the book of Hosea. Something—a comment in a sermon or Sunday school lesson—made me start looking for instances throughout the Old Testament books of prophecy where God said something about His purpose for the things the prophets were proclaiming.

Whether deliverance or destruction was in order, I noticed time and time again that God's stated purpose was that His people or the people around them might *know* that He was God. This was my first real introduction to the concept of God's justice. Of course, I'm sure I had heard it taught and preached about over the years, but there was something powerful about discovering it for myself in God's Word.

Then I got to Hosea. My pastor had preached on Hosea once, and I remember dreading the sermons during those weeks, because all I understood about the story was the horrible situation Hosea ended up in. But when I began reading Hosea with an eye towards God's justice, His mercy came blazing through along with it. Not only was God's wrath and judgment upon His people for the purpose of showing His justice, He also brought that same wrath and judgment upon them to cause them to see their sin as He saw it, that they might return. Instead of punishment, the wrath of God upon His children focused on restoration. This view of God's mercy and justice working hand in hand made the books of prophecy come alive to me in a way I never would have understood had I not read through the portions of the Bible that seemed difficult or uninteresting.

The Word of God is powerful, and every book, every chapter, every word has been purposefully chosen and included for our benefit. When we pick and choose, or read only that which is familiar, we miss much of what God has for us to learn.

When we see God's justice as it is, we begin to see our own sin as God sees it. This causes us to turn from that sin, to fight our sinful flesh, to seek to obey the promptings of the Holy Spirit more and more each day.

Justice and Injustice

As I write this, the United States of America is, on a whole, obsessed with injustice. At the forefront of our culture is a hue and cry against racial injustice, but there are many other issues of "injustice" that are being pushed into the public arena. God is just, so we too ought to be just. The problem with many of our current movements against injustice is that they seek to replace one injustice with another. A mind focused on injustice will end up treating someone else unjustly.

An example of this is the recent protests in the nearby city of Portland. While protesting injustice, these protesters destroyed public and private property, even trying to set fire to buildings. Regardless of what you may think about the cause for which they were agitating, it is a well-documented fact that the protests were anything but peaceful, and left what was once a beautiful and historic part of the city looking like a war zone.

Their passion for their cause led them into the unjust treatment of their fellow citizens, and their emotions were worked up into such a frenzy that they brought about destruction and division instead of reconciliation and resolution. This is the result of a gathering of people focused on injustice.

If we are focused on justice, we will seek lawful ways of accomplishing our goals, and our seeking of justice will be for the good of all, not just the select few. The heart from which God's justice flows is a heart of love, mercy, and righteousness. When we are setting our minds upon His justice, we will reflect His heart as well. Amid the fulfillment of God's promise of judgment on Jerusalem, Jeremiah was able to say even while mourning,

"For the Lord will not cast off for ever: But though He cause grief, yet will He have compassion according to the multitude of His mercies. For He doth not afflict willingly nor grieve the children of men." (Lamentations 3:31-33)

When our thoughts are focused on the injustice of a person or situation, our hearts will become bitter, angry, and unpitying. But when we focus on the mercy-motivated justice of God, our hearts will be filled with compassion, and a desire to forgive and restore. After all, if God can justly forgive and show mercy and compassion on you and I who have so unjustly broken His laws and treated Him with indifference, surely we can forgive and have compassion on those who have treated us unjustly.

Just View of Sin

Of course, if we are filling our minds with thoughts of God's justice informed by the Word of God, we will necessarily come to a just view of our own sin. If we can see our sin as God sees it, and remember that those *individual* sins caused Christ to die on the cross, we will see far more victory in our fight against sin.

It is no accident that the description of victory in Christ in Romans 8 follows the description of the power of sin in chapter 7. If we are to defeat our sinful flesh and quench the fiery darts of temptation aimed at us by our enemy, we must see our sin as it is: in the context of God's justice. Unless we can agree with God about the seriousness of our sin, we will not be willing to do what it takes to live in victory and reflect the righteousness of God to the wicked world around us.

That which is Just

We can certainly think upon the people whom God describes as just, and meditate upon God's own justness, but how else can we fill our minds with *"whatsoever is just"*? Remember that the word *just* has the idea of "right" or "righteous." If we are to think upon that which is just, we must fill our minds with righteousness. This necessarily means *not* filling our minds with *un*righteousness.

This is hard to do in our age of technology, with our culture constantly bombarding us with images and messages of unrighteousness. Social media, television, games, even those that purport to be "family-friendly" are filled with ideologies and images that are contrary to righteousness as God defines it. Sometimes, filling our minds with righteousness will mean saying no to things others see as "not that bad" or even "good," in order to focus our minds on things that are truly good and right according to Scripture.

Not sure where to start? Notice the things in the Bible that God specifically commends or condemns as good or wicked. Then look at your entertainment choices, the books you read, and the things you fill your mind with. Ask the Holy Spirit to show you anything He wants you to change. If you are committed to obeying the clear commands of Scripture and the promptings of the Holy Spirit, you will find your mind filled with *"whatsoever is just."*

4

⌾✥⌾

Pure

"Finally, brethren, whatsoever things are true, whatsoever things are honest, whatsoever things are just, whatsoever things are pure, whatsoever things are lovely, whatsoever things are of good report; if there be any virtue, and if there be any praise, think on these things."

Purity may be the characteristic most readily connected with this topic of bringing our thoughts into the obedience of Christ. The Greek word here for purity has the idea of being clean and innocent. It can also refer to something sacred, something that excites reverence, and paints a picture of chastity, modesty, even perfection.

If you read about the Greek and Roman cultures at the time this epistle was written, you will find that all manner of immorality and impurity was just as prevalent then as it is now. As Ecclesiastes says, *"There is no new thing under the sun."* (1:9) Even without the constant bombardment of media we have today, the temptation to dwell upon impurity was still there.

So how do we get our minds to dwell upon purity? Psalm 119 gives us a helpful clue:

"Wherewithal shall a young man cleanse his way? by taking heed thereto according to Thy Word. With my whole heart have I sought Thee: O let me not wander from Thy commandments. Thy Word have I hid in mine heart, that I might not sin against thee." (vv. 9-11)

In order to fix our minds on things that are pure, we must first fill our hearts with the pure Word of God.

"The words of the Lord are pure words: as silver tried in a furnace of earth, purified seven times." (Psalm 12:6)

"The statutes of the Lord are right, rejoicing the heart: the commandment of the Lord is pure, enlightening the eyes." (Psalm 19:8)

Every part of the Word of God is pure, and every bit of it can help us fill our minds with pure thinking. But since the entire Bible is too wide a scope for this book, let's just take a quick look at the other passages where this same Greek word for *pure* is used:

"For I am jealous over you with godly jealousy: for I have espoused you to one husband, that I may present you as a chaste virgin to Christ. But I fear, lest by any means, as the serpent beguiled Eve through his subtilty, so your minds should be corrupted from the simplicity that is in Christ." 2 Corinthians 11:2-3

The Corinthians had fallen prey to false teachers, who were maligning Paul and preaching "another Jesus" and "another gospel." (*2 Corinthians 11:4*) It is in this context of the danger of listening and accepting the false teachers and their unscriptural teachings which the word for *purity* appears.

Read through the two verses above—can you guess which is the word we're looking for?

The Greek word for *pure* used in Philippians 4:8 is translated here as *chaste*. The definition of this word has not changed much over the years since the King James Version was translated and is typically used to refer to sexual purity. Interestingly, the English word *chaste* may have originated from the concept of separation (like the word holy.) This gives us a fuller sense of the meaning of the phrase *"chaste virgin."* It is not an accidental redundancy, it is a purposeful description.

The Corinthians were part of the bride of Christ, not only made righteous through Christ's atoning sacrifice, but also set apart for Him in the same way a bride-to-be is set apart for her husband. We wouldn't think much of a woman who agreed to marry one man, but went chasing after another, even if she kept herself physically pure. Purity is not just a matter of abstaining from things that would corrupt physically: it is a matter of viewing ourselves as set apart *for* Christ.

The analogy of marriage helps us see the spiritual truth: that as Christians, we are "espoused," set apart for Christ. To allow any other influence to attract our worship and love is spiritual adultery. This truth is found throughout the Bible, including the book of James, which says,

"Ye adulterers and adulteresses, know ye not that the friendship of the world is enmity with God? whosoever therefore will be a friend of the world is the enemy of God." (4:4)

Let's apply this to our thoughts. Do we allow our minds to dwell upon things that are *pure,* in the sense of set apart for Christ, or do they reflect an affinity for the world?

Are we rooting our thinking in the Word of God, or are we soaking up the philosophies of the world?

Purity of mind means thinking on things that are morally pure, but it also means keeping our minds from chasing after anything other than God. Christ has redeemed us, paying the price for our sin with His own blood to bring us into fellowship with Him. How dare we allow ourselves to think like His enemies, when He has sacrificed so much to make us His friends!

But, of course, we are redeemed sinners who sometimes choose to sin, regardless of the victory Christ has won on our behalf. There will be times when we do not choose to dwell upon that which is pure, but God knows our weakness and has provided a way for us to get right with Him again:

"If we confess our sins, He is faithful and just to forgive us our sins, and to cleanse us from all unrighteousness." (1 John 1:9)

Not only is the blood of Christ sufficient to pay for our past sins, it is also sufficient to pay for those we have not yet committed! Of course, this does not give us permission to sin as much as we want, *(Romans 6)* but it does provide a way for us to be brought back into fellowship with God when we have strayed from Him.

This idea of repentance and forgiveness brings us to the next passage containing the Greek word for *pure*. It may be more difficult to spot in this passage, but it appears twice:

"For behold this selfsame thing, that ye sorrowed after a godly sort, what carefulness it wrought in you, yea, what clearing of yourselves, yea, what indignation, yea, what fear, yea, what vehement desire, yea, what zeal, what revenge! In all things ye have approved yourselves to be clear in this matter." (2 Corinthians 7:11)

Did you find it? It is translated here as *clear/clearing*. To make something clear, in this context, is to vindicate or prove it innocent.

The Corinthians' response to Paul's confrontation of sin in their midst was to sorrow "after a godly sort," that is, in repentance. They then did whatever it took to deal with the sin, seeking to separate themselves from it as far as possible. Where before, the wickedness in their midst had been responded to in pride, (1 Corinthians 5:1-2) they now looked upon it with humility, sacrificing a self-centered attachment to the status quo to bring the sin into the open and deal with it according to Scripture.

When we think upon things that are pure, we will seek to make our thoughts (and the heart from which they spring) right with God. That will require us to humble ourselves and confess our sinful thoughts— to choose to remember our sin to God, that He might forgive and remember it no more. *(Jeremiah 31:34)*

There is another aspect of thinking upon that which is pure. This one is found in 1 John 3, where we are told,

"Beloved, now are we the sons of God, and it doth not yet appear what we shall be: but we know that, when He shall appear, we shall be like Him; for we shall see Him as He is. And every man that hath this hope in Him purifieth himself, even as He is pure." (vv.2-3)

The hope of heaven, of eternity spent face to face with our Savior, should inspire us to greater purity in heart and mind. We will be like Christ in heaven, because we will see Him as He is. So much of our struggle with our thoughts can be traced to some deficiency in what we believe about who God is and what He is like.

Thoughts seem private, something no one else can see or know about; and yet, have you ever considered that the same Savior we will see face to face someday knows our most "private" thoughts *today?*

I have often heard the question posed: "If Christ were to come right now, what would He find you doing?" It is a valid point, and one backed up by Scripture, that the hope of Christ's imminent return can motivate us not to sin. But how much more should the fact of our one day standing before our risen Lord motivate us to be careful about our thoughts?

If Christ were to come right now, how would you feel standing before Him in the knowledge that He knew exactly what you have been thinking about?

The omniscience of God is a powerful truth to keep us careful about our thoughts, and the hope of seeing Christ face to face is a powerful source of accountability for the Christian if we choose to keep that hope fresh in our hearts and minds. This brings us back to Psalm 119:9-11 and the importance of Scripture memory.

The more of God's Word we hide in our hearts, the more the Holy Spirit has to work with when we face temptation. It is one thing to *feel* that what you are doing or thinking about is not right, it is quite another to have *God's words* brought to mind to remind you what He says about it.

Of course, our enemies love to sow seeds of impurity in our thoughts. No matter how much Scripture we feed into our minds, no matter how careful we are with what we allow ourselves to see and hear, we will all at some point have thoughts arise which tempt us away from the God-honoring thinking of Philippians 4:8.

I have heard several pastors compare this to a bird in a tree; you can't keep the bird from landing there, but you can keep it from making a nest in the branches! The appearance of a tempting thought is not sin on our part until we yield to it. Instead, it is an invitation to do as 2 Corinthians 10:5 says:

"Casting down imaginations, and every high thing that exalteth itself against the knowledge of God, and bringing into captivity every thought to the obedience of Christ"

For the saved in Christ, temptation does not equal failure. Through the power of the Holy Spirit, we can choose to submit to God and resist Satan, which causes him to flee from us. *(James 4:7)* We are in a real battle against a real enemy, but victory is already ours, so long as we are looking to God's power, not our own.

As we confess our sinful thoughts to God, ask Him for forgiveness, fill our minds with Scripture, and yield to the Holy Spirit in submissive obedience, we will find ourselves winning more and more of our thought-battles. Then we will have freedom to fill our minds with thoughts that are pure: that which is innocent, clean, and free from the stain of sin. Colossians 3:2-4 says,

"Set your affection on things above, not on things on the earth. For ye are dead, and your life is hid with Christ in God. When Christ, who is our life, shall appear, then shall ye also appear with Him in glory."

Our life is hid in Christ, and so ought our hearts and minds to be. Think on that which is pure and reject thoughts that are not, always remembering that you are set apart for Christ.

5

Lovely

"Finally, brethren, whatsoever things are true, whatsoever things are honest, whatsoever things are just, whatsoever things are pure, whatsoever things are lovely, whatsoever things are of good report; if there be any virtue, and if there be any praise, think on these things."

We tend to use the word "lovely" to describe just about anything, from a sunset or a new dress to a cup of tea. (It is used almost as widely as the word "love.") This can make it difficult to think through what Philippians 4:8 means when it says we are to think upon that which is *lovely*. A word study on the Greek word translated here as *lovely* does not help us much, because it only appears once in the New Testament. Its definition, however, does give us some insight. It means pleasing, or acceptable.

So, we are to think upon that which is pleasing or acceptable—but to whom? Are we to fill our minds with that which is pleasing to ourselves? Or is there a higher standard of acceptableness to which we are being called?

Jesus Himself defined what it means to live the Christian life in Matthew 16:24:

"If any man will come after Me, let him deny himself, and take up his cross, and follow Me."

According to this, self-denial is foundational to following Christ. 1 Corinthians 6:19-20 tells us,

"What, know ye not that your body is the temple of the Holy Ghost which is in you, which ye have of God, and ye are not your own? For ye are bought with a price: therefore glorify God in your body, and in your spirit, which are God's."

We are bought with a price: the precious blood of Christ was shed on our behalf. If ever we find that love and gratitude are not enough to motivate our obedience in the moment of temptation, we can remember that we *owe* our obedience to God as those who have been redeemed, purchased out of the slavery of sin. We are not our own, we no longer serve sin. Instead, we seek to please Christ, our perfect, loving Master.

Romans 6:16 puts it this way:

"Know ye not, that to whom ye yield yourselves servants to obey, his servants ye are to whom ye obey; whether of sin unto death, or of obedience unto righteousness?"

Whether with our thoughts or our actions, we will end up either obeying God unto righteousness, or the world, the flesh, and the devil unto sin.

1 Peter also gives us a helpful truth about following Christ:

"For even hereunto were ye called: because Christ also suffered for us, leaving us an example, that ye should follow His steps: Who did no sin, neither was guile found in His mouth: Who, when He was reviled, reviled not again; when He suffered, He threatened not, but committed Himself to Him that judgeth righteously: Who His own self bare our sins in His own body on the tree, that we, being dead to sins, should live unto righteousness: by whose stripes ye were healed." (2:21-24)

From this we can see that following Christ means following His example. It may mean suffering, just as He suffered; and it will entail living out the reality that we are dead to sin, and alive to righteousness.

What does this mean for our thoughts? It certainly means that *Christ* is to define what is and is not acceptable and pleasing, since it is *His* example we are seeking to follow, *His* righteousness we are seeking to live out. Our thoughts will be "lovely" when they fall in line with the righteousness of God.

This passage also reminds us that the Christian life is one of sacrifice. To say yes to God's righteousness necessarily means we must say no to unrighteousness, however much we would rather say yes at the time.

The bringing of our thoughts captive to the obedience of Christ requires us to choose to act upon the reality that we are dead to sin. It requires that we yield to the Holy Spirit, laying down our own will in order to embrace His.

Of course, Jesus is the perfect example of this, who said, *"And He that sent me is with Me: the Father hath not left Me alone, for I do always those things that please Him." (John 8:29)*

So you see, the Christian's mission is to please God, just as Jesus did, and to choose His will over our own. This applies to our thoughts as well as any other area of life. To think upon things that are lovely means to think upon things *Christ* would find pleasing and acceptable.

If you and I are truly committed to thinking upon that which is lovely, we will be willing to deny ourselves, refusing to let anything less than lovely into our minds, no matter how pleasing that thing might seem to our flesh.

As with each of these qualities, it takes a purposeful choice to train our minds upon that which is lovely, but God promises us His grace when we humbly seek Him. James 4:6 tells us,

"But He giveth more grace. Wherefore He saith, God resisteth the proud, but giveth grace unto the humble."

As we make those daily, constant choices to keep our thoughts striving after God's approval, He will give us grace to follow through on each choice. However, the opposite is also true: if we are refusing to obey God in what we welcome into our thoughts, that very act of pride will cause God to resist, or oppose us.

Obedience in our thinking is just as important as obedience in our actions. Throughout Scripture, we can see that God pours out His grace abundantly on those who humbly seek to please Him.

So, who are your thoughts aiming to please today?

6

✦

Of Good Report

"Finally, brethren, whatsoever things are true, whatsoever things are honest, whatsoever things are just, whatsoever things are pure, whatsoever things are lovely, whatsoever things are of good report; if there be any virtue, and if there be any praise, think on these things."

What does it mean for something to be *"of good report?"* When I initially looked this phrase up in my Strong's concordance, the definition said, "reputable, well-spoken of." That gave me a little better picture of what this means, but it wasn't until I looked up the two Greek words joined together to make the compound word translated as *"good report"* that the lightbulb came on for me.

The first of these two words simply means "good." While the compound word in Philippians 4:8 only appears once in the New Testament, this word "good" appears a total of five times, and I found it quite enlightening to see just what kind of "good" Philippians 4 is talking about.

Three of the gospels use this word "good" in their record of Jesus' parable of the nobleman who went into a far country, leaving three of his servants a specific sum to keep on his behalf. When he returned, he found that two of his servants had managed what they were given faithfully:

"His lord said unto him, Well done, thou good and faithful servant: thou hast been faithful over a few things, I will make thee ruler over many things: enter thou into the joy of thy lord." (Matthew 25:21)

This verse is often quoted in terms of our own day of reckoning with our Master. We would all like to hear our Lord say *"Well done, thou good and faithful servant"* one day. But think about what makes a good servant: obedience, faithfulness to do what we're told. A good servant of God is one who obeys Him.

In Mark 14:7, Jesus is addressing those who objected to the "waste" of ointment Mary of Bethany had just poured out over Jesus in an act of love and worship. He responded to their indignation by saying,

"For ye have the poor with you always, and whensoever ye will ye may do them good: but Me ye have not always."

Acts 15:29 also uses the same word, translated here as "do well," when recounting the decision of the Council of Jerusalem not to require Gentile believers to fulfill the law of Moses, asking only,

"That ye abstain from meats offered to idols, and from blood, and from things strangled, and from fornication: from which if ye keep yourselves, ye shall do well. Fare ye well."

And Ephesians 6:3 instructs children to obey their parents,

"That it may be well with thee, and thou mayest live long on the earth."

What's my point in stringing these verses together? Simply to give us a fuller picture of what the "good" in "good report" means: for one to be good, do good, for it to be well with someone—all of these point to a complete goodness, a goodness that has no bad mixed in. The faithful servant is not commended because he did adequately, or because the good he did outweighed the bad. A good report will not be a mixed review.

To give a practical example from my own life, let's consider books. I love being able to recommend books to people, but there are many books I would not recommend without a caveat. The book as a whole may be good, but even one mention of something that might cause someone to stumble is enough to keep me from giving that person a "good report" of that book.

Now, let's look at the word translated *"report."* It occurs just twice in the New Testament, both in the gospels. In Matthew 9:26, Jesus has just raised a little girl from the dead, and, understandably, we are told that

"the fame hereof went abroad into all that land."

In Luke 4:14, Jesus returns from His victory over Satan's attempts to tempt Him to sin.

"And Jesus returned in the power of the Spirit into Galilee: and there went out a fame of Him through all the region round about."

On both of these occasions, "fame" went out: a report was spread that Jesus had done and was doing amazing things. A good report is the "fame" or reputation for goodness that goes out from something. Just a note of application here: what kind of report goes out about you and me? Are we living out the goodness of God so faithfully that it becomes our defining characteristic?

Our thoughts should dwell on that which is *"of good report."* This means that we should *not* be filling our minds with that which has a reputation of wickedness. This may be as simple as being selective in which news reports you read, or it may be as delicate and complex as choosing to distance yourself from a friend who constantly tells you negative things about other people.

The Bible is clear in condemning the sin of gossip, but it permeates our homes and churches nonetheless. At its core, gossip is the opposite of a "good report," and God is not pleased when we allow gossip to dwell in our minds. What we think about eventually comes out of our mouths, and one of the reasons gossip can be such a struggle for us is that we often choose to let our minds shelter thoughts of things that are simply none of our business.

Consider the following verses:

"Thou shalt not go up and down as a talebearer among thy people: neither shalt thou stand against the blood of thy neighbour: I am the Lord." Leviticus 19:16,

"A talebearer revealeth secrets: but he that is of a faithful spirit concealeth the matter." Proverbs 11:13

"The words of a talebearer are as wounds, and they go down into the innermost parts of the belly." Proverbs 18:8; Proverbs 26:22

"He that goeth about as a talebearer revealeth secrets: therefore meddle not with him that flattereth with his lips." Proverbs 20:19

"Where no wood is, there the fire goeth out: so where there is no talebearer, the strife ceaseth." Proverbs 26:20

Oftentimes, the temptation to gossip comes when we happen upon information we have no Biblical reason to know about. Whether by accidentally overhearing, or being told a gossipy detail by someone else, it is easy to accidentally gain knowledge we have no right to.

Gossip causes so much destruction in families, churches, and friendships; and if you're reading this book, you probably wouldn't set out on purpose to destroy anyone. But what do we do when we accidentally stumble across information we have no business having? How should we respond?

Pray. Gossipy information in the back of our minds is like having a sore spot in your mouth that your tongue just can't leave alone. That situation will probably resurface in your mind almost constantly for a while, and the best thing to do is to use each of those thoughts as a prompting to pray. God already knows all about the situation, and He has all the information on every part of the matter. Nothing is hidden from God.

You can also ask God for wisdom in deciding what to do with the information you have. Such matters are rarely clear-cut, and you will need God's leading, wisdom, and discernment to know whether God wants you to act upon the information in some way, or simply to pray for those involved.

Dismiss the thoughts as quickly as possible. If God isn't prompting you to do something about the situation, and if you are neither part of the problem nor of the Biblical solution, it is your responsibility not to harbor those thoughts which will otherwise come out of your mouth as gossip. Women especially are made for communication, and we have a natural urge to share whatever fills our minds with our friends and family. We have a responsibility to make sure that the things we allow to stay in our thoughts are things of good report.

Refuse to hold grudges or let the information affect your attitude towards those involved. If I have no right to information, and there is no Biblical course of action required, I have no right to pick up an offense toward those involved. This is often where the battle becomes the most fierce. Whether or not we feel others deserve it, you and I have a responsibility to show the love of Christ to *everyone* around us—especially those we know are struggling in some way.

Like Christ, we should never condone sin or ignore problems the Holy Spirit is calling us to address; but also like Christ, we need to have a heart of compassion and forgiveness to others.

Whatever the wrongs of others, the second you or I harbor bitterness or unforgiveness in our hearts, that is sin. We cannot change what others have said or done, but we can control our own response to the situation. We must forgive *as Christ forgave us.*

This Christlike attitude of the heart can be the first step towards healing in a situation. As you accept God's grace to respond properly, He may lead others to you who likewise need to accept God's grace.

Perhaps the information God has allowed you to have is for the purpose of behind-the-scenes intercession through prayer, or an appropriate word of counsel, or even just a greater sensitivity to the needs of those the situation touches. Whatever it is, you will need to listen to (and obey) the Holy Spirit's leading. As you do, you will see God do a work, first in your heart, then in the hearts and lives of others. That is the power of thinking upon things that are *of good report* and refusing to think upon that which is not.

7

Virtue

"Finally, brethren, whatsoever things are true, whatsoever things are honest, whatsoever things are just, whatsoever things are pure, whatsoever things are lovely, whatsoever things are of good report; if there be any virtue, and if there be any praise, think on these things."

Virtue isn't something we talk much about these days. If anything, our current culture has given the word a negative connotation. But virtue appears in this list of things God Himself wants us to think about. But what is virtue, and how do we fill our minds with it?

Definition:

The Greek word translated *virtue* here is only used a few times in the Bible. It has the literal meaning of "manliness," and is derived from the Greek word for man. But it is also said to have the sense of moral excellence. Curious, I did some research and found that in Greek culture during the New Testament era, this word had come to be used to describe something that is fulfilling its specific purpose. (That's where the idea of *excellence* comes in.)

Biblically speaking, this fits together quite well. God made man to glorify Him. God is glorified by moral excellence; therefore, when (through the power of the Holy Spirit) a man demonstrates moral excellence, he is fulfilling the purpose for which he was made.

Now, in our current culture, the tendency would be to look at this word and be offended at it for being gender specific. Yet, there is a Biblical foundation for this as well:

"For Adam was first formed, then Eve" (1 Timothy 2:13)

There is no reason to be offended at this call to think on those things that have to do with virtue in the sense of manliness, because we know that God established gender on purpose, and that He has a purpose for every word in Scripture.

In our present culture, the call to fill our minds with moral excellence is important, but it also goes hand in hand with the idea of manliness. As I write this, there is a definite and deliberate push in our culture towards the transgender movement and the general watering down of gender differences.

Whether it's TV, movies, commercials, billboards, or even children's picture books, the idea of manliness in particular has all but disappeared in the flood of gender confusion. As Christians, we have the responsibility to fill our minds, not with the world's concept of gender, but with that which exemplifies *God's* design.

It is interesting to me that the Greek root of the word translated *virtue* here is found in Christ's teaching against divorce in Mark 10:6.

"But from the beginning of the creation God made them male and female."

God's purposeful creation of male and female is a foundational truth that forms the basis for marriage, family life, and even the structure and practice of the local church. Take away gender distinctions, and church, family, marriages, and society at large disintegrate. It is important to keep in mind the Biblical definition of manliness.

It is, of course, valuable for men to fill their minds with things that exemplify how God designed them to fulfill His purpose in being men; but it is equally important for women to be intentional about what we fill our minds with in this area. I could give examples of characters from movies and books who give us an unbiblical conception of what a man ought to be, but it is probably more in keeping with Philippians 4:8 to show us instead a few passages that describe qualities of "virtuous" manhood as God defines it.

"Husbands, love your wives, even as Christ also loved the church, and gave Himself for it" Ephesians 5:25

"Likewise, ye husbands, dwell with them according to knowledge, giving honour unto the wife, as unto the weaker vessel, and as being heirs together of the grace of life; that your prayers be not hindered." 1 Peter 3:7

"Rebuke not an elder, but intreat him as a father; and the younger men as brethren; The elder women as mothers; the younger as sisters, with all purity. Honour widows that are widows indeed." 1 Timothy 5:1-3

"For a bishop must be blameless, as the steward of God; not selfwilled, not soon angry, not given to wine, no striker, not given to filthy lucre; But a lover of hospitality, a lover of good men, sober, just, holy, temperate; Holding fast the faithful word as he hath been taught, that he may be able by sound doctrine both to exhort and to convince the gainsayers." Titus 1:7-9

These are just a few passages, but they give us a starting point. We are to fill our minds with things that demonstrate, exemplify, or inspire these qualities. This can be difficult, especially in our entertainment-saturated society. It may mean setting aside some of your favorite books and movies, but isn't that worth it in the grand scheme of developing a mind that thinks the way God thinks?

So far, we've only dealt with the part of the definition that has to do with manliness, but what about moral excellence? I think the basic principle is the same, as it is with each of the qualities listed in Philippians 4:8. We need to commit ourselves to focusing wholeheartedly on that which is excellent in the sight of God.

When I think of moral excellence, I think of the fruit of the Spirit in Galatians 5:22-23, or the description of charity in 1 Corinthians 13. For us women, the obvious passage on excellence would be Proverbs 31. Another passage dealing with excellence actually contains this same word for *virtue*.

It's a lengthy chunk of Scripture, but worth careful reading:

"Grace and peace be multiplied unto you through the knowledge of God, and of Jesus our Lord,

According as His divine power hath given unto us all things that pertain unto life and godliness, through the knowledge of Him that hath called us to glory and virtue:

Whereby are given unto us exceeding great and precious promises: that by these ye might be partakers of the divine nature, having escaped the corruption that is in the world through lust.

And beside this, giving all diligence, add to your faith virtue; and to virtue knowledge;

And to knowledge temperance; and to temperance patience; and to patience godliness; and to godliness brotherly kindness; and to brotherly kindness charity.

For if these things be in you and abound, they make you that ye shall neither be barren nor unfruitful in the knowledge of our Lord Jesus Christ." (2 Peter 1:2-8)

Notice first that God has *called* us to virtue. As with the other qualities with which God commands us to fill our minds, we are also called to *be* virtuous. Our actions flow out of our thoughts, so if our thoughts are filled with God's definition of moral excellence, we will be more likely to act accordingly. –And isn't that the point?

Notice also that virtue is just the second "step," so to speak, of the walk of faith. The foundation for moral excellence in our lives is faith. And this ties together everything we have seen in this chapter regarding virtue. If we believe that God created us male and female, we will seek to live out His purpose and design in creating us as He has.

Our concept of manliness (and femininity, for that matter) will be rooted in what we believe about God. If we believe that God is Who He says He is, we will yield to Him as the absolute standard of morality, and our idea of moral excellence will flow out of that which He defines as morally excellent.

The opposite is also true: If we believe the lies of the world, the flesh, and the devil regarding gender, or morality, we will act upon those beliefs, and the result will be devastating, for, *"the way of transgressors is hard." (Proverbs 13:15)*

Before we move on to the last quality given in Philippians 4:8, I want to take you to just one more verse. 1 Peter 2:9 also contains the Greek word we have been discussing, but here it is translated as *praises.*

"But ye are a chosen generation, a royal priesthood, an holy nation, a peculiar people; that ye should shew forth the praises of Him who hath called you out of darkness into His marvellous light"

This verse is significant because it reminds us that any virtue we see here on earth, any excellence any human being possesses or demonstrates, is ultimately for the purpose of showing *God's* virtue, His excellence.

Virtue of heart, mind, character, and action are crucial for the Christian, because they are the way we show forth the virtue of God Himself. Virtue in the Biblical sense sets us apart from the world as God's own people, specifically belonging to Him, reflecting His light in the darkness of a lost and fallen world.

8

⚜

Praise

"Finally, brethren, whatsoever things are true, whatsoever things are honest, whatsoever things are just, whatsoever things are pure, whatsoever things are lovely, whatsoever things are of good report; if there be any virtue, and if there be any praise, think on these things."

In a way, this last characteristic of God-honoring thought could be viewed as a summary of those listed before it. The word translated *"praise"* has the meaning of something praiseworthy, "concretely commendable," as Strong's puts it. The word appears eleven times in the New Testament, always translated "praise" in the sense of approval or approbation.

In the 1 Peter 2 passage dealing with governmental authorities, we are told,

"Submit yourselves to every ordinance of man for the Lord's sake: whether it be to the king as supreme; Or unto governors, as unto them that are sent by Him for the punishment of evildoers, and for the praise of them that do well."(vv.13-14)

Similarly, Romans 13:3 states,

"For rulers are not a terror to good works, but to the evil. Wilt thou then be afraid of the power? do that which is good, and thou shalt have praise of the same"

In 2 Corinthians 8:18, the word praise is applied to a believer.

"And we have sent with him the brother, whose praise is in the gospel throughout all the churches"

Aside from these three occurrences, the word is primarily used in relation to the praise of God, or God's praise or approval of Christians. In the midst of explaining the difference between the letter and the spirit of the law in Romans 2:29, the parenthetical statement is given,

"whose praise is not of men, but of God."

In other words, it is God who sees the heart, so it is God who ultimately bestows true praise or approval. 1 Corinthians 4:4-5 also emphasizes this truth.

"For I know nothing by myself; yet am I not hereby justified: but He that judgeth me is the Lord. Therefore judge nothing before the time, until the Lord come, who both will bring to light the hidden things of darkness, and will make manifest the counsels of the hearts: and then shall every man have praise of God."

To fill our minds with "praise" means to dwell on those things that are worthy of praise, approval, or approbation in the sight of God. What are those things? A good way to begin training our minds to recognize and choose praiseworthy thoughts is simply to read the Bible and notice when God gives something His approval. For example, Psalms 133:1 says,

"Behold, how good and how pleasant it is for brethren to dwell together in unity!"

If we are filling our minds with discord and strife (whether real-life or in fiction,) we are not choosing what God says is good and pleasant. Matthew 5 also gives a number of statements, often referred to as "the beatitudes," having to do with character qualities Jesus Himself calls "blessed." As we look at what God defines as praiseworthy, we will be better able to recognize and choose to fill our minds with those things.

I am reminded of 2 Timothy 2:15, which says,

"Study to shew thyself approved unto God, a workman that needeth not to be ashamed, rightly dividing the word of truth."

We should be striving for God's approval. It should be our top priority, our most pressing goal. The world around us seeks the approval of peers, celebrities, or the far-flung world of social media followers. But God's children are called to be different. We have a perfect, holy Father who not only is pleased when His children obey from the heart, He has given us His own Spirit to enable us to do that which is pleasing to Him. As Philippians 2:13 reminds us,

"For it is God which worketh in you both to will and to do of His good pleasure."

There is another aspect to the New Testament's use of the word "praise." It is that we, as we do that which pleases God, become conduits of *His* praise. Jesus illustrated this dynamic well in Luke 17:10.

"So likewise ye, when ye shall have done all those things which are commanded you, say, We are unprofitable servants: we have done that which was our duty to do."

We are servants of God, not laboring for our own glory or good, but for God's. We do that which pleases our Master because it is our simple duty as a servant. And yet, because it is God we serve, that duty is (or should be) motivated by a heart of love and worship.

Take for example the elders of Revelation 4:

"The four and twenty elders fall down before Him that sat on the throne, and worship Him that liveth for ever and ever, and cast their crowns before the throne, saying, Thou art worthy, O Lord, to receive glory and honour and power: for Thou hast created all things, and for Thy pleasure they are and were created." (vv.10-11)

Whatever heavenly rewards or accolades our obedience may earn will in turn be given back to God, for it is He alone who is worthy of glory and praise. It is in this context of glorifying God that we find the rest of the occurrences of the word "praise" in the New Testament.

Earlier in Philippians, we find the following:

And this I pray, that your love may abound yet more and more in knowledge and in all judgment; That ye may approve things that are excellent; that ye may be sincere and without offence till the day of Christ; Being filled with the fruits of righteousness, which are by Jesus Christ, unto the glory and praise of God." (1:9-11)

There is much in those three verses, but notice that Paul's prayer centers around Christlike character and actions, with the understanding that these things are only possible through Christ, and for the purpose of God's glory and praise. The first chapter of Ephesians also gives us several verses dealing with this same idea, with the repeated phrase "to the praise of His glory." The following passage is lengthy, and without getting bogged down or sidetracked by the word "predestined," notice with me what it is that is said to be to the praise of the glory of God:

"Blessed be the God and Father of our Lord Jesus Christ, Who hath blessed us with all spiritual blessings in heavenly places in Christ:

According as He hath chosen us in Him before the foundation of the world, that we should be holy and without blame before Him in love:

Having predestinated us unto the adoption of children by Jesus Christ to Himself, according to the good pleasure of His will,

To the praise of the glory of His grace, wherein he hath made us accepted in the beloved.

In whom we have redemption through His blood, the forgiveness of sins, according to the riches of His grace;

Wherein He hath abounded toward us in all wisdom and prudence;

Having made known unto us the mystery of His will, according to His good pleasure which He hath purposed in Himself:

That in the dispensation of the fulness of times He might gather together in one all things in Christ, both which are in heaven, and which are on earth; even in Him:

In whom also we have obtained an inheritance, being predestinated according to the purpose of Him who worketh all things after the counsel of His own will:

That we should be to the praise of His glory, who first trusted in Christ.

In whom ye also trusted, after that ye heard the word of truth, the gospel of your salvation: in whom also after that ye believed, ye were sealed with that Holy Spirit of promise,

Which is the earnest of our inheritance until the redemption of the purchased possession, unto the praise of His glory." (vv. 3-14)

In my Bible, I have those three occurrences of the word "praise" circled. Each one has to do with an aspect of what Christ has purchased and ordained for the believer. The first one, is our adoption as children of God. (v.5) The next refers to our inheritance in Christ, bestowed on us by Christ that we should be to the praise of His glory. (v. 11-12) The last mention of the word praise connects it with the Holy Spirit, given to us as earnest, or proof of His purchase and our redemption.

God will ultimately be glorified by our lives as we live out the truth of who we are in Christ: children, heirs, dwellingplaces of the Holy Spirit Himself! As this study comes to an end, my question for you is, are you willing to yield your thoughts (and consequently, your deeds) to God? Are you willing to fight your natural inclination and choose to let the Holy Spirit change your thoughts and make your heart and mind a fit dwelling for His presence?

To think thoughts that are praiseworthy in the sight of God will take intentional choices moment by moment. It will take a constant awareness of what you are thinking and what *God* thinks of what you are thinking. It will take work, but if you have trusted Christ as your Savior, God has already given you the power, strength, and ability you need to conquer your thoughts and build habits of righteousness in your thinking. As 1 Peter 3:11 says, "*eschew evil, and do good.*" Yield today to the Holy Spirit's conviction and leading regarding your thoughts.

You won't regret it!

"*Finally, brethren, whatsoever things are true, whatsoever things are honest, whatsoever things are just, whatsoever things are pure, whatsoever things are lovely, whatsoever things are of good report; if there be any virtue, and if there be any praise, think on these things.*"

www.ingramcontent.com/pod-product-compliance
Lightning Source LLC
Chambersburg PA
CBHW060355130626
46553CB00003B/1243